The Simple Guide to Great Photography

The Simple Guide to Great Photography

EASY TIPS & TRICKS
for Photographing Children, Family, Pets, Cars & More!

by April Bryant

HPP MEDIA & DESIGN

Printed in the United States of America

First Printing

All Images © April Bryant *(unless noted)*

ISBN pending 0692546030

Requests for permission to make copies of any part of the work should be sent to:

HPP Media & Design
Bybee, TN
info@hoipolloipx.com

www.AprilBryant.com
www.HoiPolloiPhotography.com

CONTENTS

PREFACE

Over the years, I have had many people ask for advice in improving their photography. Some were new photographers, on their way to being professionals. But, most were just regular folks who didn't want to have to take a photography course to decipher the technical mumbo-jumbo of most photography or camera manuals. They just wanted to be able to make good photos of their kids, in most instances.

If you are someone who wants better photos, right now, with simple, easy to follow techniques, this book is for you! I promise to keep the mumbo-jumbo to the bare minimum, and to give you information that is truly helpful and understandable.

I know when I first started getting interested in photography, way back in the dust, before there was an internet (yes, I'm that old!) I would have loved to find an easy to understand guide of simple basics, tips, and tricks to improve my photographs. So, I decided to write this book of the quickest and easiest ways to make better photos, along with some easy to read basics.

I have included, in this book, a basic camera guide, composition pointers, and tips on photographing the most commonly requested subjects like children, family, pets, cars, travel, and more!

As a bonus, I have included a Quick Reference chart with a link so you can download it as a .pdf and store it on your smartphone.

INTRODUCTION

Your photographs. Your precious memories. Moments you can never get back. Most of the time you won't have a professional photographer at the ready when those precious seconds elapse. In fact, most often, when you do have a photographer, the scene is fake or set-up. As a professional photographer, I can tell you that real moments, real smiles, real laughter, or even tears, will be far more meaningful, years from now, when you flip back through your family album.

One of my favorite photos from this family shoot. The mom had just snatched up this handsome little guy in a playful hug. That is pure happiness, completely unstaged.

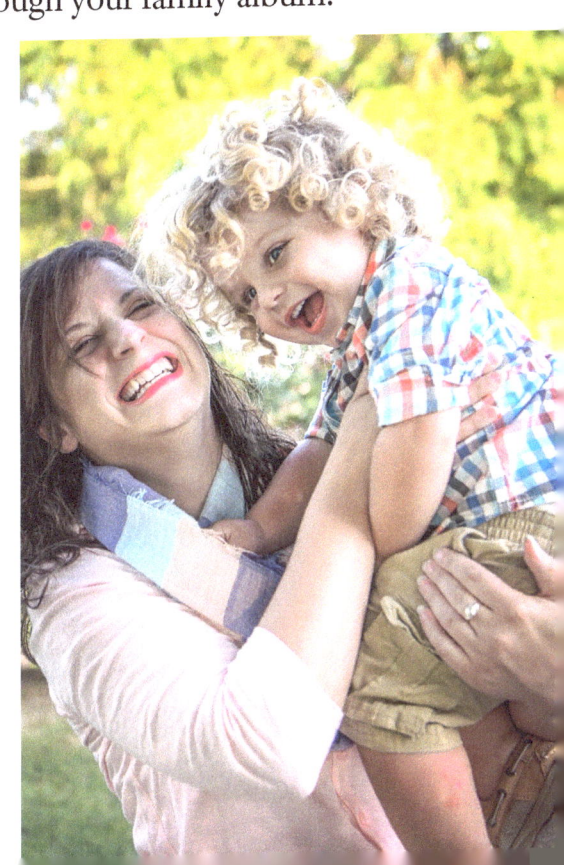

As a matter of fact, I specifically prefer not to "pose" clients in a studio environment, but instead take them outside and let them play or interact, naturally. I love capturing parent/child moments where they really are talking, hugging, playing, laughing, or enjoying themselves, and I want to show you how you can do that, too, as well as how to get great photographs of the most common subjects.

Why am I writing this book, and telling you how it's done? I want to share my knowledge with you because I think everyone deserves to have really wonderful images that they can treasure and pass down to the next generations. The simple tips provided in this book, will allow you to do that. I guarantee, if you follow the simple methods outlined here, you will see a major improvement in your photos.

I decided a few years ago that I was going to scan all of our family photos, and date, tag, and add as much info as we could to each image. Some of my treasures happen to be tin-types of my Great-grandmother and great-great grandfather that were made around 1900. That turned out to be a project that lasted three years! As I scanned and tagged, we kept finding boxes or albums of photos. It was quite the undertaking! Final count was over 8,000 images, but with each one, I noticed things and I learned things.

Yeah, those studio shot photos were nice, well focused, and composed properly, but I much preferred the candid family photos where something was really happening, not just a collective group in front of a gaudy 70's backdrop (Oh, some of those were awful!).

This is not your typical photography book, filled cover to cover with jargon and technical terms and diagrams that might act as a sedative for your average non-professional photographer. My intention with this book is to provide everyday folks some quick and easy techniques to take better photos, even with their phones!

So, why wait? Let's get started making your memories spectacular!

Tin type photos of my great-grandmother and great-great grandfather circa 1900. (Photographer Unknown)

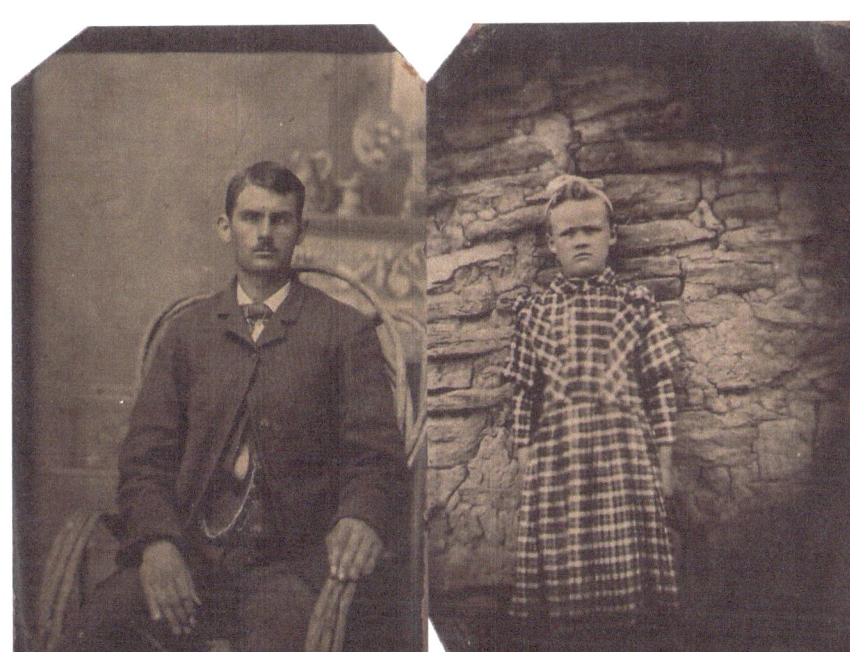

1 • YOUR CAMERA

First and foremost, you don't have to have an expensive camera to make great photos. Let me say that again for those in the back. You don't have to have an expensive camera to make great photos.

In fact, professional photographers are quite offended on a regular basis by people remarking, "Your photographs are so beautiful. You must have a great camera!" Which, is the equivalent of telling Emeril that his food is amazing, so he must have a great stove. Ouch!

Believe it or not, this sweet photo of my neighbor's grandson was made with an iPhone 5. It was one of those rare occasions when I didn't have my camera with me, and I just couldn't let that precious moment go by.

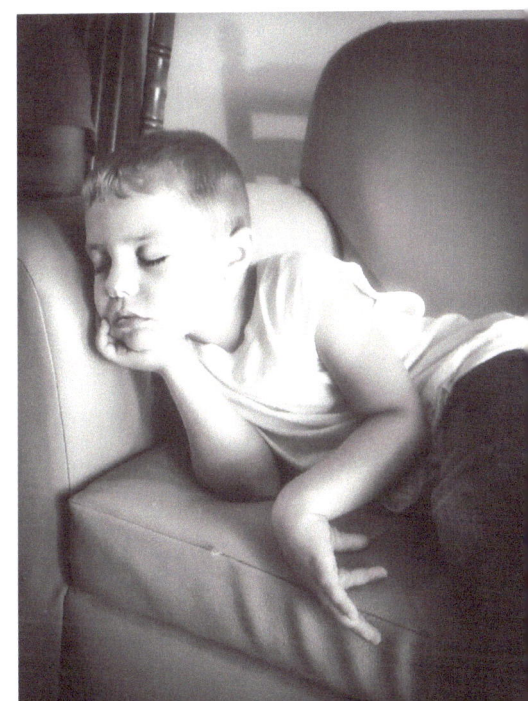

It helps to have nice equipment, but if you don't know how to use it, you aren't gaining any ground.

Let's take look at some of the types of cameras.

DSLR

At the high end of the spectrum are the DSLRs. What does DSLR stand for? Digital Single Lens Reflex. What does that mean? Well, I promised not to bore you with technical terms, jargon, and diagrams. But, suffice to say, they have a mirror that moves to allow light to reach the sensor. Going into more of that would break my promise. If you want to know more, a quick Google search will yield enough info to put you to sleep forever.

DSLRs have a full range of settings, and if you are the proud owner of one, I highly recommend really learning how to use it to its full capacity. That, however, is beyond the scope of this book.

Mirrorless or DSLT

What does DSLT stand for? Digital Single Lens Translucent. What does that mean? They have a translucent mirror that is fixed and does not move. Because of this, they are cheaper to produce. There have been some amazing advancements in this technology, and there are mirrorless models show-ing up at the high end of photography these days.

Point & Shoot

These are a part of the aforementioned DSLTs, but I wanted to give them a separate category because these are probably the most common cameras (excluding phones) for non-professional photog-raphers. They often have quick and easy automatic settings. This is the type of camera I bought for my mom who wants to take nice photos but doesn't want to do much more than pushing the shutter button.

Point & Shoot cameras usually have a nice range of functions, and you can choose (hopefully, while reading this book) which ones will yield the results you are looking for and which ones you want to try. I recommend practicing around the house and being comfortable with new settings, before changing settings in an environment where you don't want to miss a moment.

Camera Phones

Boy, have these come a long way from the awful pixelated images of just a few scant years ago! Some phones are as capable as a nice Point &

Shoot of capturing great images. In fact, there are some very talented photographers out there using nothing but iPhones. With the latest release, there are even more adjustable settings, as well.

Digital Zoom vs. Optical Zoom

While we are on the subject of cameras, I'd like to take a moment and explain the difference between digital zoom and optical zoom. Both have a feeling of getting you closer to a subject, but there is a big difference.

Optical zoom is a true zoom, using the glass in the lens to magnify the subject. Digital zoom is not a true zoom, as it only enlarges a portion of what you are seeing, thus the more you zoom with digital zoom, the more quality is lost.

So, if you can, it's better to move closer to a subject instead of using digital zoom. You can always crop a photo down with editing software or an editing app.

Summary

- You don't have to have an expensive camera to make great photos.
- DSLR–has movable mirror, more expensive

- DSLT–fixed translucent mirror, cheaper to produce
- Point & Shoot–most common (excluding phones), easy to use
- Camera Phones – some now have more advanced features
- Digital Zoom – not a true zoom, just enlarging, loses quality
- Optical Zoom – true zoom using optics

Whatever camera you choose (or already have), know that you can get great photos by applying the techniques in this book. So grab your camera! You are ready to move on to the next chapter.

2 • THE PHOTOGRAPHIC TRIANGLE

This is another topic for which you can Google till your heart's content. But, for the purposes of this book, and not to make you fall asleep, here is the quick and over-simplified version.

Photography literally means "the study of light." The following three factors determine the results from your camera and balancing the three creates great images.

ISO

What does ISO mean? Funny story. ISO literally means International Standards Organization, borne into use by the photography industry as it referred to the sensitivity of film to light. Older folks will remember film cameras and buying typically 200 ISO film for slower moving or still subjects, and 400 ISO film for sports or fast moving subjects.

With the invention of digital cameras, the term remains, but the beauty is that you don't have to buy a roll of film for a specific use. You could actually change the ISO for every photo you take digitally (provided your camera has that option).

As with film in the old days, the higher the ISO the more "noise" (graininess) your photograph will have, but as the ISO goes up, so does your ability to make photos in darker environments.

Aperture

This is the term for the size of the opening of the lens to allow light through to the sensor. It's personally my favorite way to control photographs by creating depth of field (DOF). Depth of field is how in or out of focus the background of your subject is.

Aperture is measured as f-stops, and without going into a math lesson, just remember that smaller numbers are larger apertures. For example, f/22 is a much smaller opening than f/2.8. The wider the aperture (smaller number) the more isolated your subject will be because more of the background is blurred (referred to as a shallow depth of field).

Grab your camera manual and check to see if your camera has a way to change the aperture and

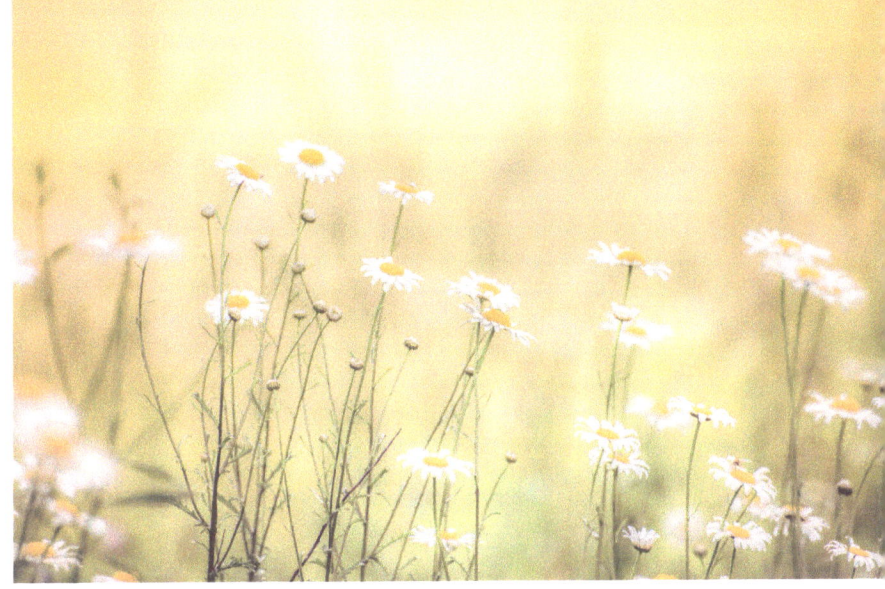

This photo illustrates how you can isolate a subject (even from an entire field of grass) with a wider aperture (smaller number).

practice with it. Try the lowest setting and the highest setting. Be creative and explore!

➜ Using a wide aperture (f/5.6 or lower) when photographing a group can be a challenge. A nice starting point for that situation is f/8. Review your photos and make sure everyone is in focus and move to a smaller aperture like f/11, f/16, or f/22 if necessary.

Shutter Speed

Just as it sounds, this is how fast the shutter opens and closes. Faster speeds are great for sports and action shots, but remember the faster the shutter opens and closes, the less light gets to the sensor. Try this setting on your camera and explore it as well.

Summary

- Photography is the study of light.
- Photographic triangle is composed of ISO, aperture, and shutter speed.
- ISO – sensitivity to light
- Aperture – the size of the opening of the lens to let in light.
- Shutter Speed – how fast the shutter opens and closes.

With practice, you can figure out the settings that work best for you and you will have the knowledge of what happens when you change each one.

3 • COMPOSITION

Composition is a very important part of making your photographs look great. I want to give you the things I regard as priorities when composing my shots.

The Rule of Thirds

The rule of thirds is a process of dividing a photograph (for our case, but applies to art designs, paintings, and even video) into 9 equal parts—think tic-tac-toe board. Important subjects should be placed at the intersections.

Imagine your photo with this grid. You want to put the most important parts of the photo in the areas of the red circled targets.

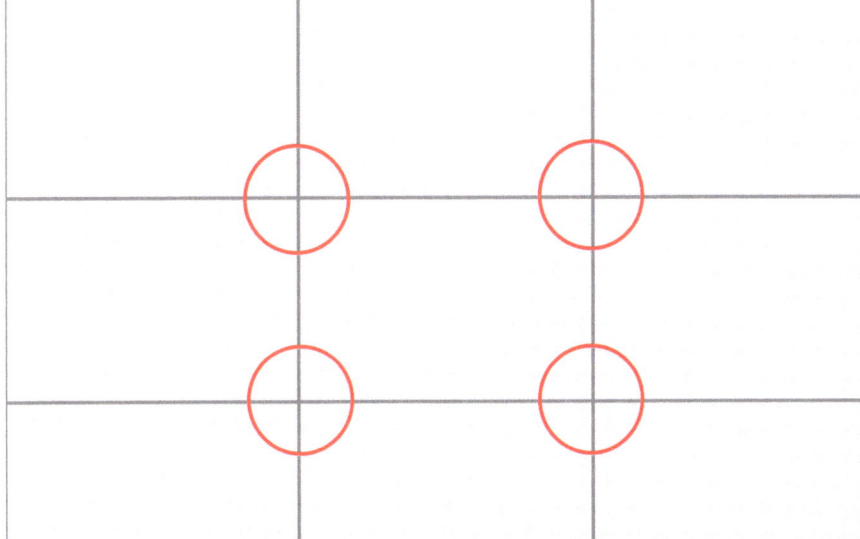

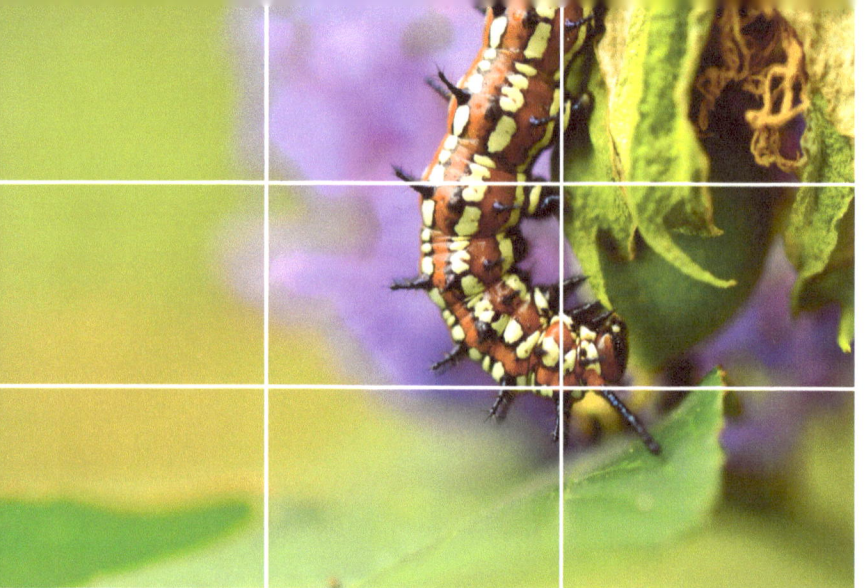

Rule of thirds example 1: In this example, you can see the caterpillar's head is in the area of the lower right intersection.

If the subject takes up more room in the photo, they should fall along one of the lines, either vertical or horizontal. Also the horizon line in a landscape

Rule of thirds example 2: In this example, note that the parakeet's eye in the area of the upper right intersection.

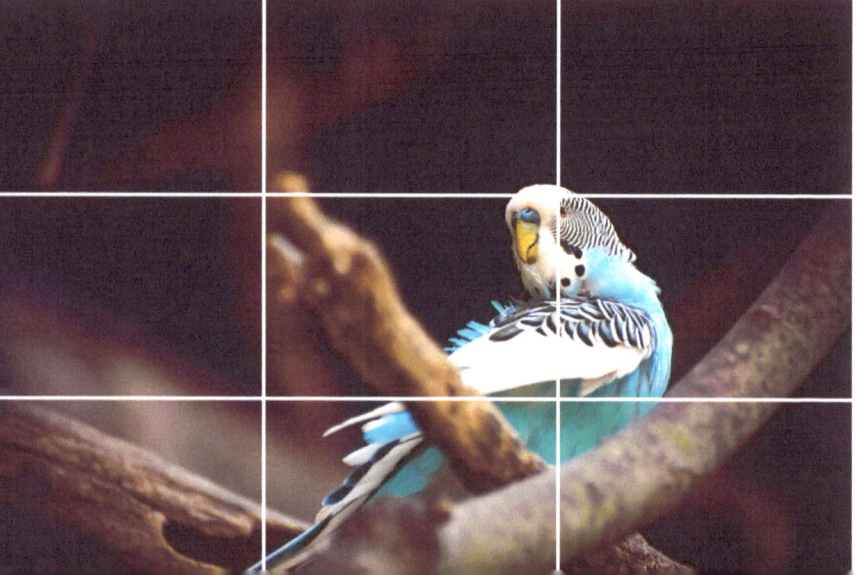

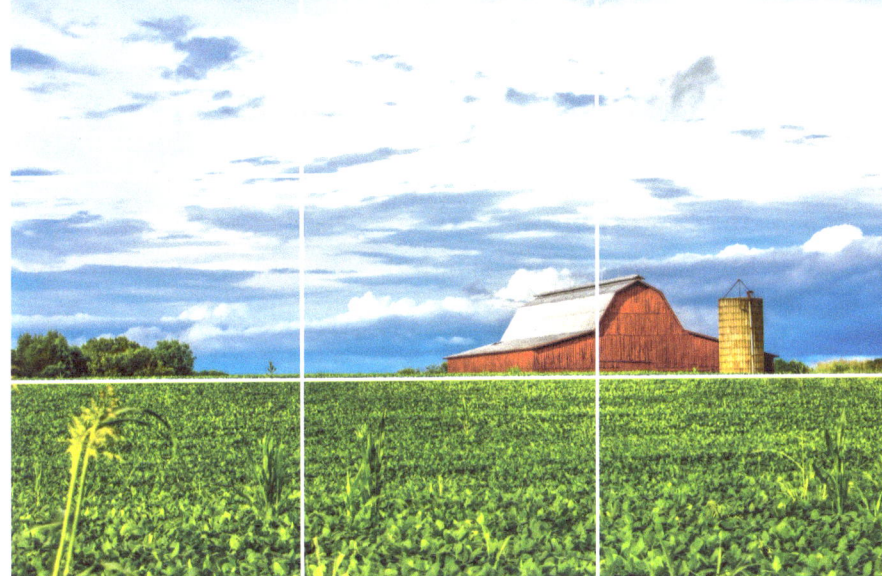

Rule of thirds example 3: In this example, you can see two aspects of the rule of thirds. The barn is near the lower right intersection, and the horizon lies along the bottom line.

shot should fall on one of the two horizontal lines, to have it dead center is not ideal. Actually, to have anything dead-center in a photograph loses interest visually in most cases. The exception is if you are going for a totally symmetrical look for something such as a water reflection.

Keep It Simple

Too much going on in a photo is a distraction. Try to minimize your photos to isolate your subject clearly. A good way to do this is to imagine what you are seeing through the camera as a photo on your wall, try to eliminate extra space. This is a great situation to use that wide (lower number) aperture to blur out the background.

The Eyes Have It!

If you are photographing people or animals (possibly even potatoes...ha!) always, always, always make sure the eyes are in focus. The first thing people see are the eyes when looking at another person. You don't want the first thing they see in your photo to be blurry. It ruins the whole image, no matter how good the rest of it is.

I am often shocked when looking at portraits that have been "professionally" done, only to see blurry eyes. It makes a huge difference in how much better your photos will look.

How could it be anything else, with such beautiful, angelic eyes? Also note the rule of thirds as she is not centered in the frame and the use of depth of field (a lower number aperture) to blur the background and really make her darling face stand out.

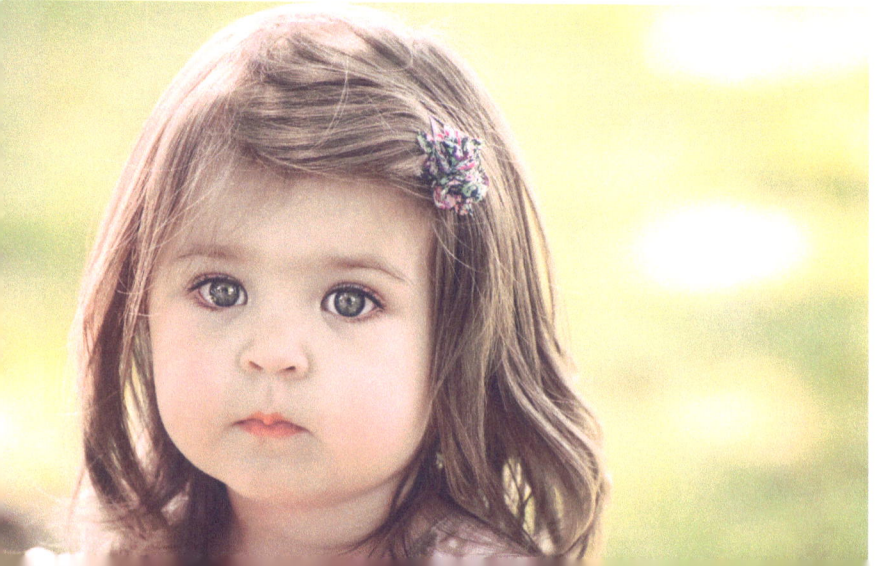

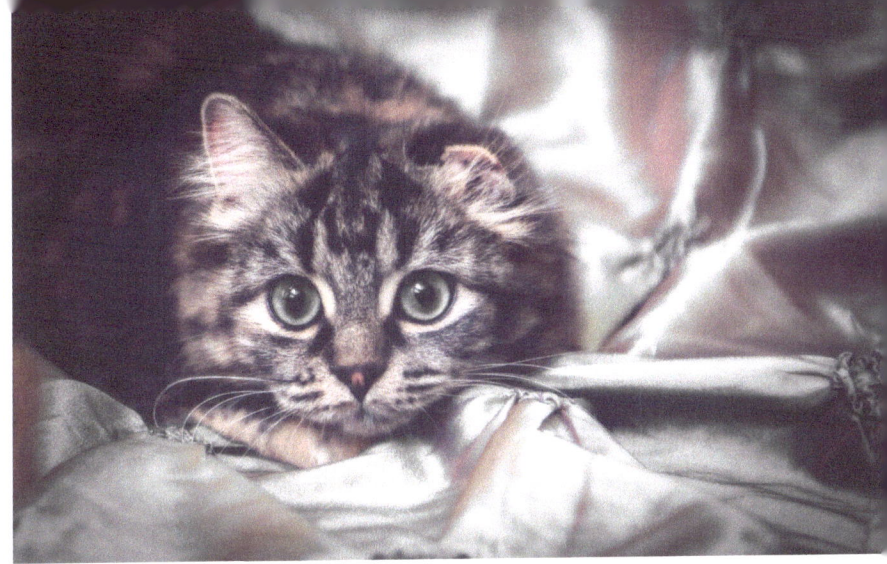

This image is all about the eyes. Note that they are the only thing in the image in perfectly sharp focus.

Somewhere to Go

When photographing people, sports, or automobiles, the photo is more pleasing if you give your subject some space "to go," or where, at least, your eye can perceive that the subject would have been a few frames later. When doing portraits, if the subject isn't looking at the camera, it is nice to give some space to where it appears they are looking, if not, it appears they are looking at something that you cut out of the image and it's a bit frustrating for the viewer.

Framing

No, not like sending someone to jail for something they didn't do, but a nicer, friendlier framing. If you have the opportunity to add something (a lot of times, a tree branch) to the edges of your photograph, it will add some nice visual interest

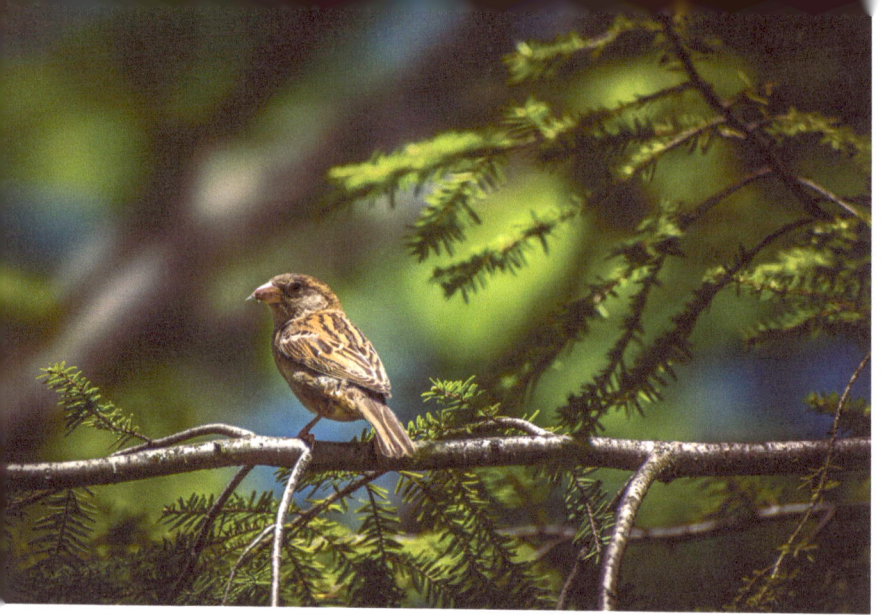

In this image, the bird is framed nicely by the tree branches.
Look for creative ways to incorporate framing into your photos.

and give your photos a very polished look, especially when combined with the rule of thirds.

Balance of Light

I once had an art teacher explain in balancing light that if you took the photo or painting and converted it to black and white and took out all the black and all the white that it took to make the range of tones from black to gray to white that a balanced photo or painting would result in equal amounts of black and white.

There are a couple of exceptions to this rule artistically, called high-key and low-key photography.

High key photography uses mid-tone gray to bright white and reduces shadows to the extreme.

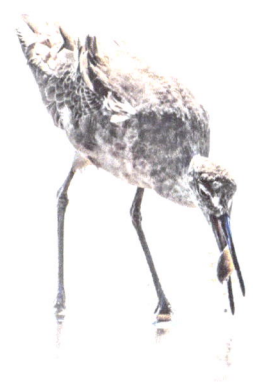

This photo is an example of high-key photography. Note that the darkest areas are only a gray color, not completely black.

In contrast, low-key photography makes the most of dark tones and shadows to create very dramatic images.

This photo is an example of low-key photography. Note how dark tones are used to make the subject stand out and create dramatic contrast.

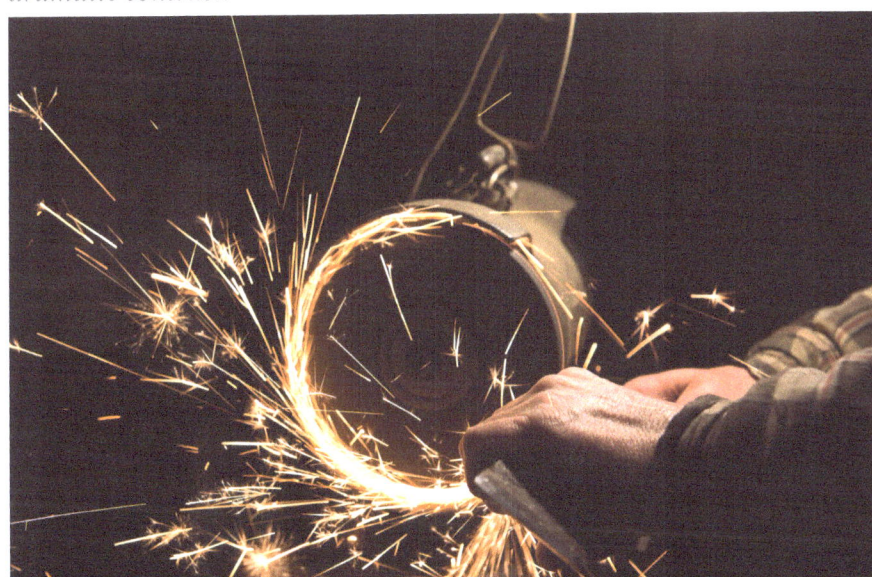

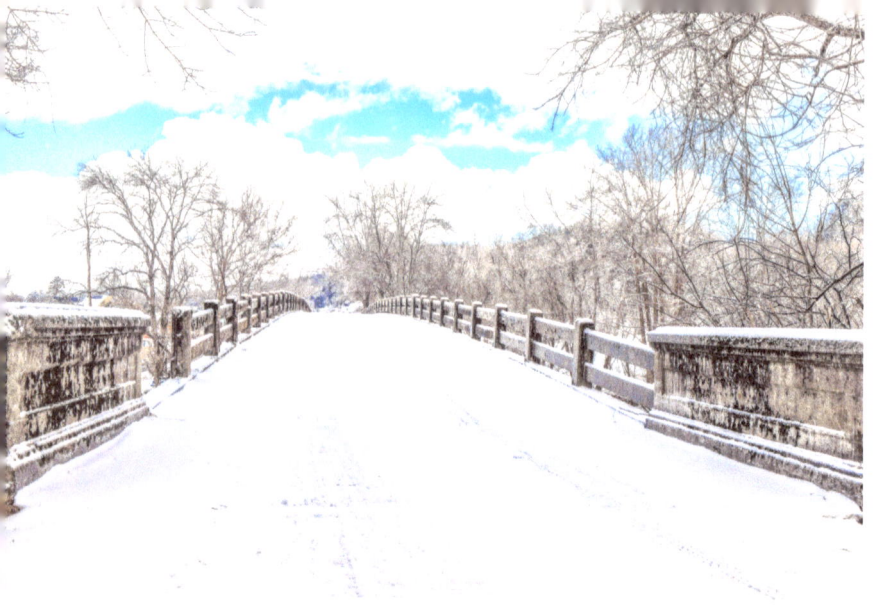

Leading Lines

Leading lines are a way to draw your viewer into your photo. Roads, pathways, fences, and train tracks are some examples. They should lead the viewer's eye into your photo, much like they were actually walking through the scene.

The two photos on this page show examples of leading lines. Note how they draw your eye visually through the image.

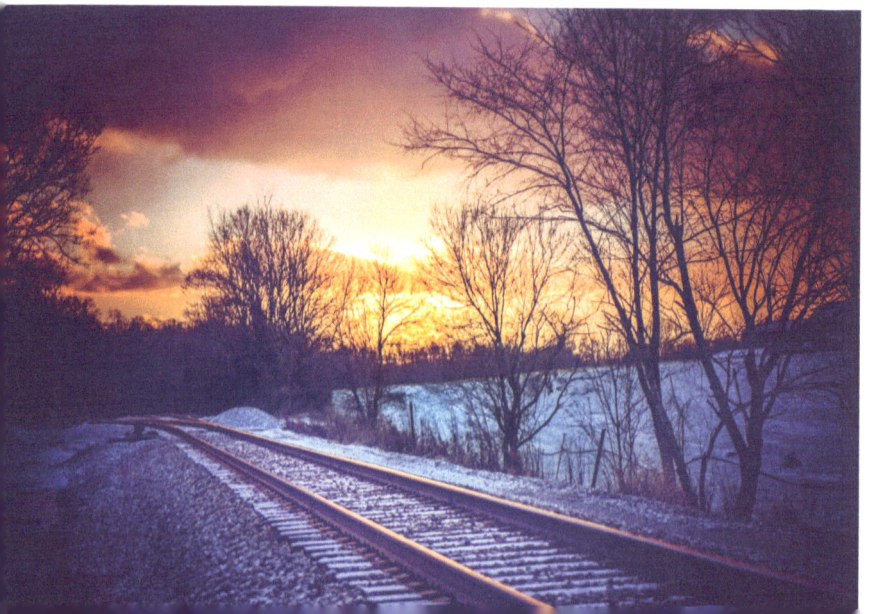

Bokeh

What is bokeh, and how the heck to you say it? Bokeh is a blur of light created by the lens, and I say BOH-ka (though I think there are several accepted ways to say it). You can create some beautiful effects with bokeh, especially if your background has a lot of lights or sparkles.

In order to create bokeh, you will need a wider aperture to cause more blur to the background. A great place to practice is in front of a Christmas tree or strands of lights. Place your subject a few feet in front of the lights, and set your aperture as wide (smaller number) as your camera will allow. Move things closer and farther from the lights to see the different effects.

This photo was created using a potted tulip and a string of Christmas lights behind a thin white backdrop using a wide aperture. The result was a nice, sparkling, spring composition.

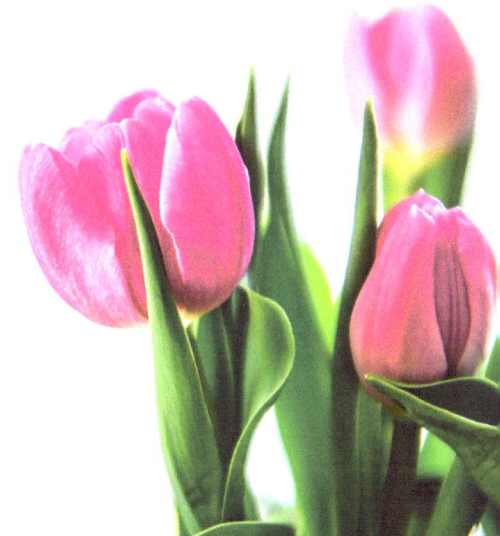

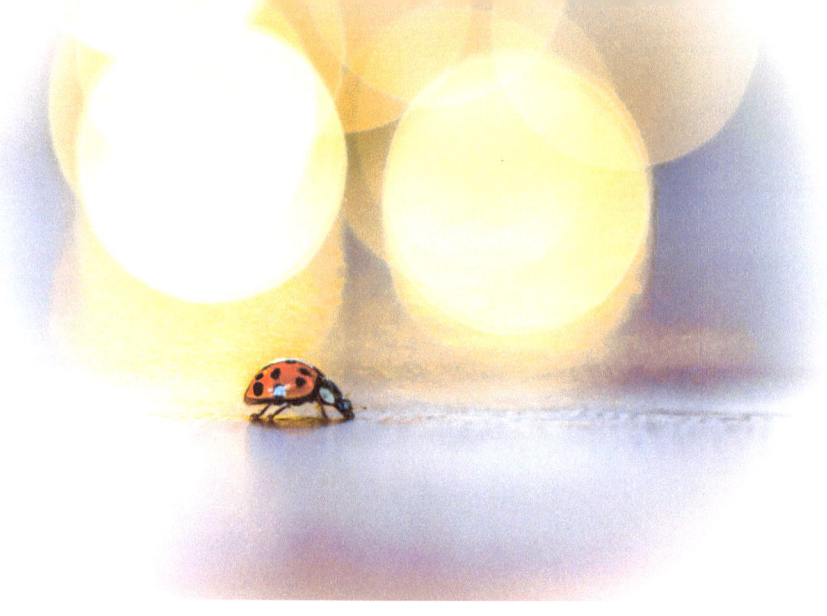

This photo was also created using a string of Christmas lights behind a wayward ladybug who wandered into the house.

You can create some really interesting photos using bokeh. It can add a lot of extra sparkle to holiday and birthday card photos. Don't be afraid to try it. It's an easy way to add a professional touch.

Summary

- Don't forget, the rule of thirds is always your friend.

- Straight horizon lines are a must.

- Try to keep your composition as simple as possible.

- If your subject has eyes, make sure they are in focus!

- Give your subject somewhere to go or a place to look.

- Look for creative ways to frame your image.

- Keep balance of light in mind for the type of photo you want to achieve.

- Use leading lines to draw your viewer into your composition

- Create magic with bokeh by using a wide aperture

Composition can make or break an otherwise nice image. Applying these rules will make your photos shine!

4 • LIGHTING

As I mentioned already, photography is really all about light. So, as you might imagine, lighting plays the major role in what you are going to get out of your camera. Finding the light is what successful photographers do best. Books upon books have been written solely about lighting, but my mission in this book is to keep things simple and as easy as possible.

Most people tend to think of natural light/outdoor or window light and flash or studio lighting when the subject of lighting comes up.

Natural Light

I love natural light! It's much easier to get nice photos with less equipment when using daylight, and you don't have to have an intimate techical knowledge of artificial lighting setups. That said, midday light with a subject in full sun is one of the most challenging photo situations you will run into, so having an awareness of how light affects your photos is very helpful, especially since natural light is not something you can control.

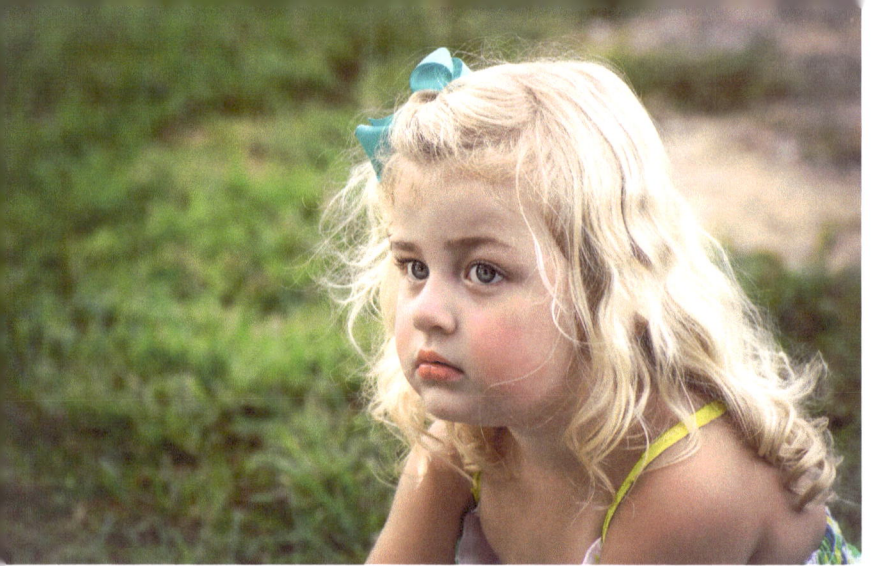

This portrait was made outdoors with only natural light.

If at all possible, you will want to move your subject into open shade, solid shade is best, because I would classify dappled shade just as difficult as full midday sun. Dappled light will cause unsightly shadows and blotches on people's heads and faces that would take hours of editing to resolve.

The midday sun can cause some weird issues, such as noses casting shadows on a smile, which can look like your subject is missing a few teeth! If you are shooting midday, think about using some props, such as a patio umbrella if you are at the beach or poolside, or use a regular umbrella, included in the shot sometimes creates interest, or just out of the shot, only used to deflect those harsh rays and minimize shadows.

➜ I almost always wear a white shirt when doing outdoor portraits. It acts as a reflector for light and helps brighten the eyes and face of my subjects without using artificial lighting, which leads to our next topic.

Flash

There are all sorts of off-camera light set-ups, soft-boxes (cloth box made to diffuse studio lights), and professional lighting, but you wouldn't be reading this book if you wanted to go to that much trouble. After all, this is a book about getting better photos with simple tips and techniques. So, we will just focus (see what I did there?) on the flash that is likely made into your camera or phone.

On camera flash is pretty harsh light. Another issue is that we are used to looking at people with over-head light, either from interior light or the sun. When the light comes from our camera, we see people in a different light, literally! Think of those campfire stories with the flashlight under your chin for that ghoulish, scary look—same concept! Only, "ghoulish" is probably not the look you are going for the majority of the time.

In some situations, especially indoors, in dark set-tings, using flash will be unavoidable. But, here's where that larger aperture (lower number) will allow more light into your camera, and where you might be able to turn up the ISO to a higher number to get the photo. A little noisy (grainy) is better than not getting the photo at all, or it being so blurry that no one even knows what it is.

One of the best places to use that on camera flash is outdoors in natural light. The flash can help lighten those harsh midday shadows in bright light, referred to as fill lighting. Bet you never thought one of the best places to use your flash was in bright sun, but it's true!

Again, I encourage you to experiment with this as cameras and phones are different and some are easier and more forgiving than others, so it pays to know what your camera captures before you actually need it for important photos.

Golden Hour

I can't possibly give you tips on lighting without mentioning "golden hour." It's the time of day that photographers live for, the hour after sunrise and the hour before sunset. These two hours usually provide the most beautiful, warm, and soft light of the day. Harsh shadows are gone and there is often a gorgeous highlight, especially on hair that will give your photos a very professional look.

Golden hour's softer light also helps eliminate subjects having to squint their eyes. It's not a good look

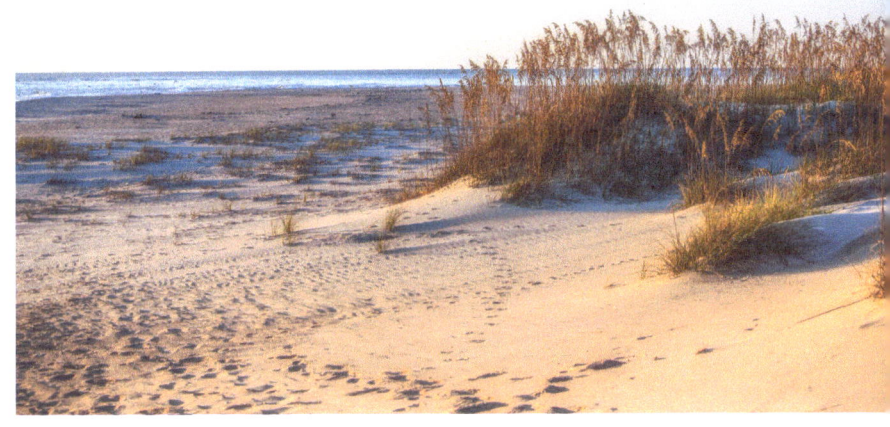

This photo was taken during the morning golden hour on Bald Head Island, NC. Note how warm the light is and the soft shadows.

for anyone; so if you notice your subjects squinting, try turning them away from the bright light.

If you have the time and your subjects are willing, a nice way to find the best light is to have them turn slowly 360 degrees while you observe where and how the light falls on them most beautifully. It's a nice and easy way to find your best light.

Something else to keep in mind is that front lighting, meaning the light source is in front of the subject, helps to minimize textures, such as wrinkles or blemishes. Side lighting enhances these things because it casts a small shadow where they occur. Being aware of that will also help you make more flattering photos, and people usually appreciate that!

Blue Hour

The hour immediately before sunrise and immediately after sunset is called the blue hour. There is a bit of light available and it is a lovely time to make "night shots." A lot of photos that appear to have been shot when it is totally dark, have actually been shot at blue hour.

Sometimes to get good blue hours shots, you will need a tripod or a way to hold your camera perfectly still, such as propping it on something solid. If you can master the challenge, blue hours shots can be very impressive!

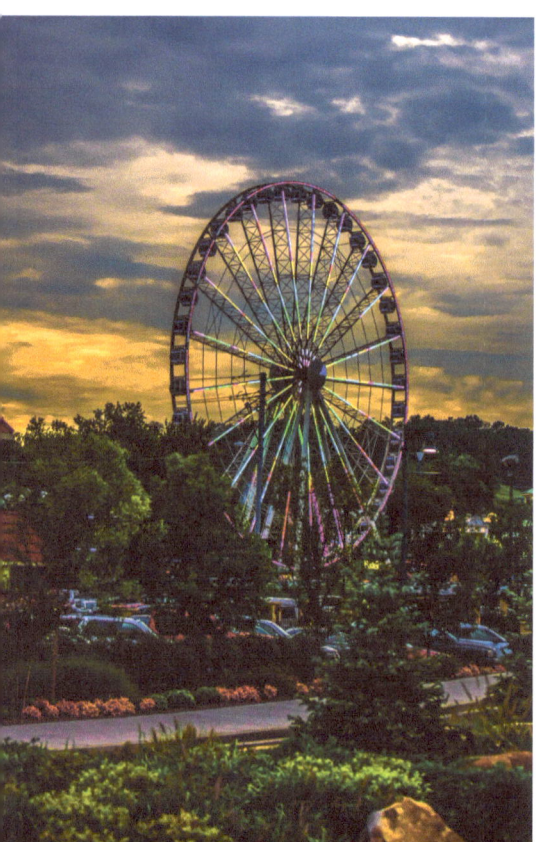

This photo was taken as golden hour slipped into blue hour. Note how interesting the lights become as blue hour approaches.

Summary

- Light plays a major role in what you get from your camera
- Natural light requires less equipment
- Place subjects in open shade if possible
- Use umbrellas to diffuse harsh light
- Avoid dappled light
- Use flash for fill light to soften harsh shadows in bright sunlight
- Golden hour – beautiful soft, warm light, great for portraits
- Blue hour – great time to make night shots

Master the light and master your shot. Remember to study the light, where it shines, how bright it is, when it's most beautiful. Light is the key element of photography.

5 • YOUR SUBJECTS

There are millions of subjects out there, but I want to give you pointers on the most common subjects that a non-professional photographer will likely encounter or want to know more about.

Children

I'm betting that the majority of the readers of this book are parents who want to be able to capture better photos of their children, so I'll start with those little cuties.

As a photographer, I am begging you, please don't ask them to fake smile. Kids are real, very real, and a fake smile is so cheesy. If you pay attention, you will notice that kids will laugh while they are playing, but they don't really smile all that much. So when you ask your kids to smile for a photo, it often doesn't really look like them.

My approach when photographing children, I always explain to my clients, is much like wildlife photography. I say this, and it's funny, but it's also true! You have to let them get used to you being

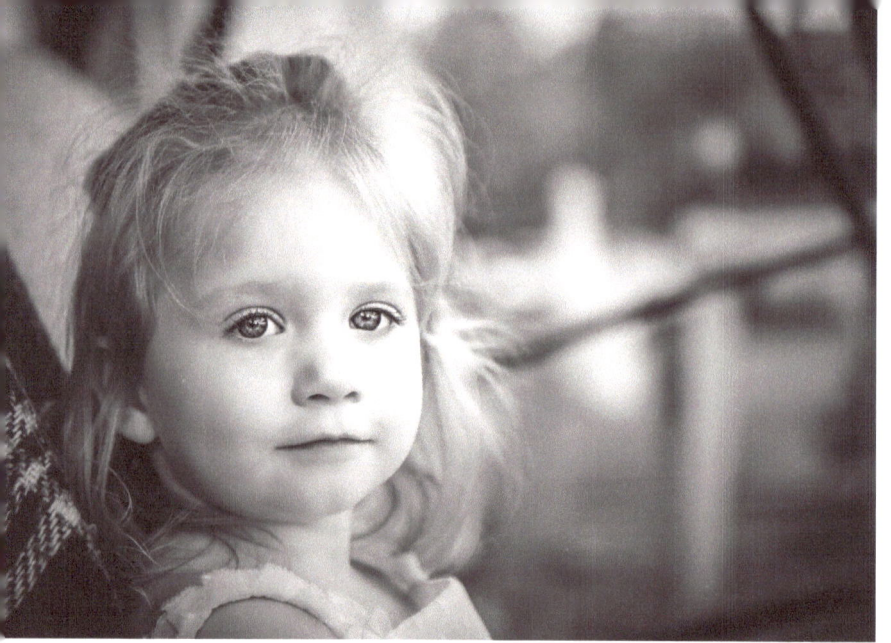

Natural expression photos are so much better than cheesy fake smiles.

there with a camera, and let them act natural. Those are the photos that are going to look like your children.

Also, don't be afraid to get in close to them, and get down on their level. Far away photos won't give you those shots with personality. Play with them while you make photos and make it fun. Then you will be able to catch those real laughs and special moments.

Families

Building on what we just discussed about children, family photos also look best when they happen naturally.

I love to take families out, during golden hour, of course, to a beautiful location, preferably somewhere that all directions have a nice background so I can just let them interact normally. Creating a playful atmosphere takes the pressure off everyone having a forced smile. After a few minutes of play, they will almost forget I am there and that's when the magic happens. The best shots are never set up, only captured.

Have parents carry their smaller children and walk with them. Restless little ones will be much happier moving and you won't end up with photos of them squirming to get down or crying. When parents are walking while holding them, they are

This family photo was taken on a shoot that was a lot of fun for everyone. Golden hour light in a beautiful location allowed these parents to just play with their children instead of posing.

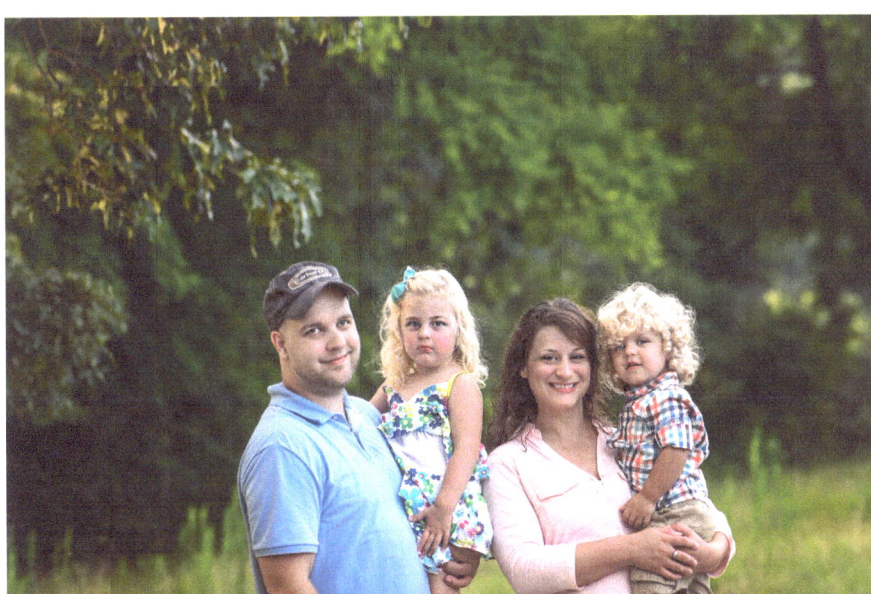

much more content and it's an easy way to get great family group photos.

Pets

Our pets are members of our families, so we certainly want great shots of them. While some are very cooperative and friendly, others are fast moving, and challenging. This creates a range of getting great photos of them from really easy to nearly impossible.

It helps tremendously to have a pet wrangler help you in keeping their attention with favorite toys or treats. It pays to be ready; the best shots often come unexpectedly.

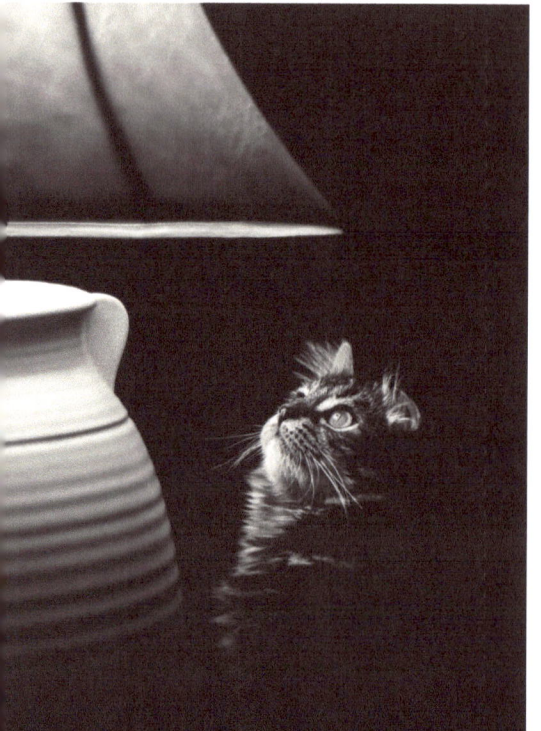

This is our cat, Gracie, and what you can't see is that there was a fly inside that lampshade that completely held her attention for just a few seconds. The lamp was the only light on in the room, and thank goodness my camera was close at hand, and I didn't miss this great shot.

Sports

In sports situations with fast action, you will want to move your ISO setting up to a higher number, try ISO 400 and also increase the shutter speed if your camera has that capability. A wider aperture can also be helpful, just remember that the wider opening (smaller number) will blur the background so be sure where you are focused.

Automotive

One of my favorite subjects, because you can get really creative! Some of the first photography I did was of show cars. Getting low, even to the point of lying down on the ground, if you dare, can yield some nice shots. Shooting from one of the four corners is a great angle or point of view.

This photo was taken from a low point of view from one of the corners so you can see the front as well as the side of the car.

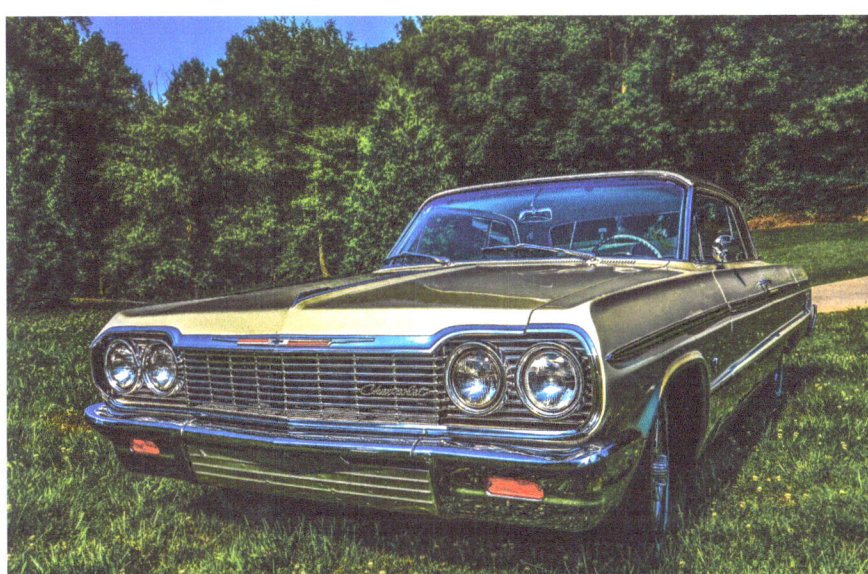

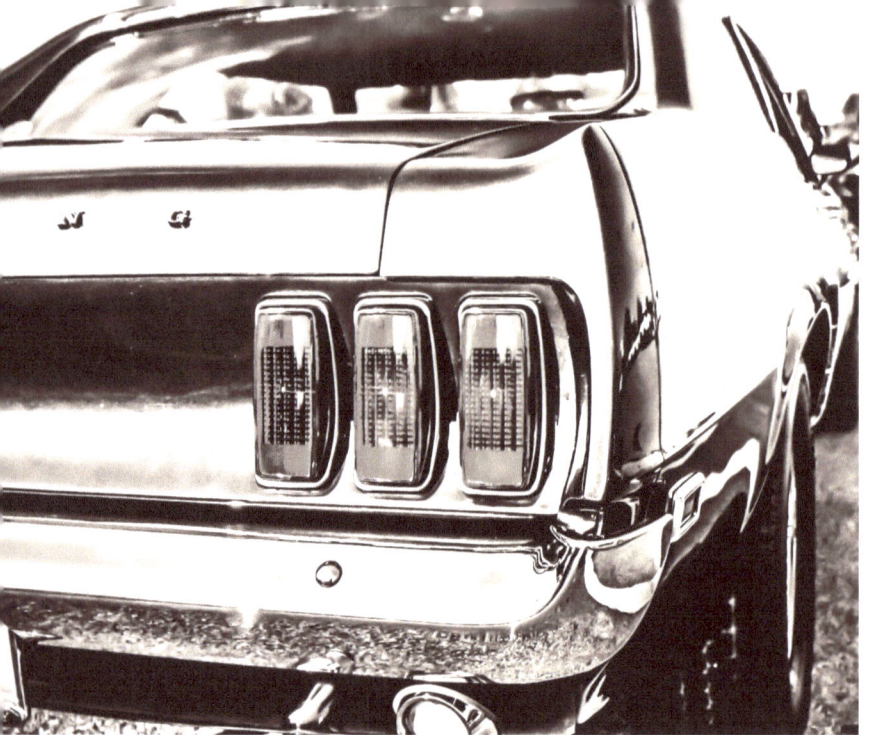

This photo of iconic taillights is one of my most popular images. It has won several awards.

Make sure that you aren't cutting off parts of the car if your intent is to make a photo of the entire automobile. Also, as mentioned in the section on composition, don't forget to give the car some space –somewhere to go.

Try odd angles and photographing smaller parts of the car, like just the taillights, or steering wheel, the grill or iconic emblems. Be bold!

Landscapes

One of the most important tips I can give you with landscape photography, and it makes the biggest

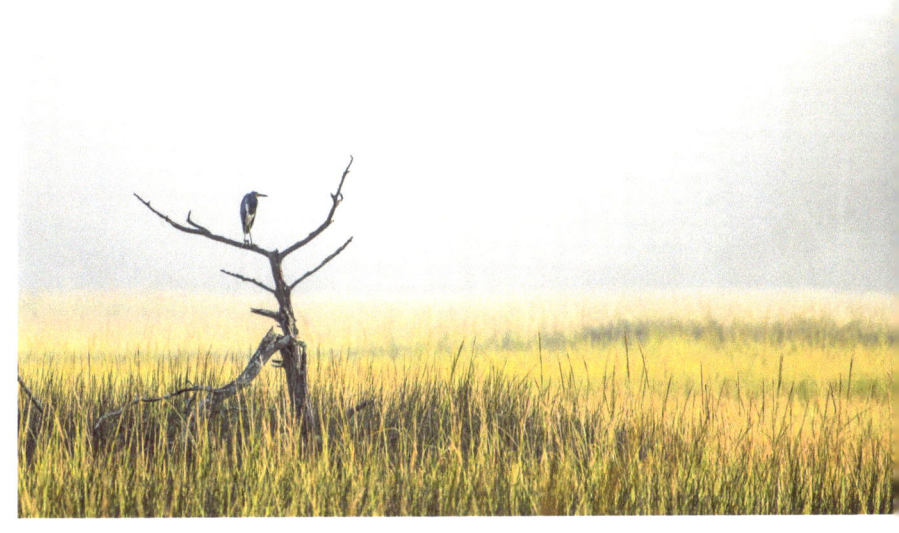

This photo was taken during the morning golden hour on Bald Head Island, NC. Keeping the horizon line level is important to the quality of the photo.

impact, is to make sure to keep your horizon line straight. A diagonal horizon line will absolutely ruin an otherwise beautiful landscape photo. Also keep in mind the rule of thirds for that horizon line. It should fall on one of the lines unless you are specifically trying to put it in the center for creative purposes.

Travel

It sometimes proves difficult to "capture" the spirit of the location where you are traveling and we often try to get everything in a single photo. Face it, that is next to impossible in most instances. I'm not saying to leave out those wide, sweeping landscapes showing your location, but my advice

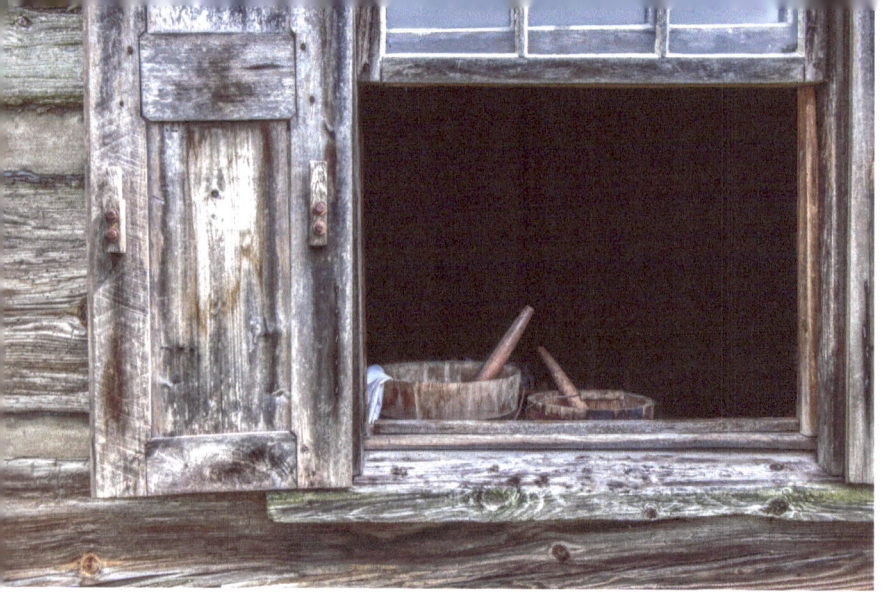

Smaller scenes like this one from historic Crockett Tavern in Morristown, TN, sometime give a better impression than trying to capture too much in one image.

is to also work on a smaller scale and find scenes or objects that have the feeling of the place. Try to make your photos show a small "slice of life" instead of an attempt to show your entire vacation/ travels in one or two images.

Macro

Macro photography typically means close-up or larger than life views of small things, such as insects or flowers. It can be a very rewarding genre, because it allows viewers to see things they might not be able to see. It's like looking through a microscope.

A lot of times, you can achieve a very interesting abstract photo by getting really close. Some

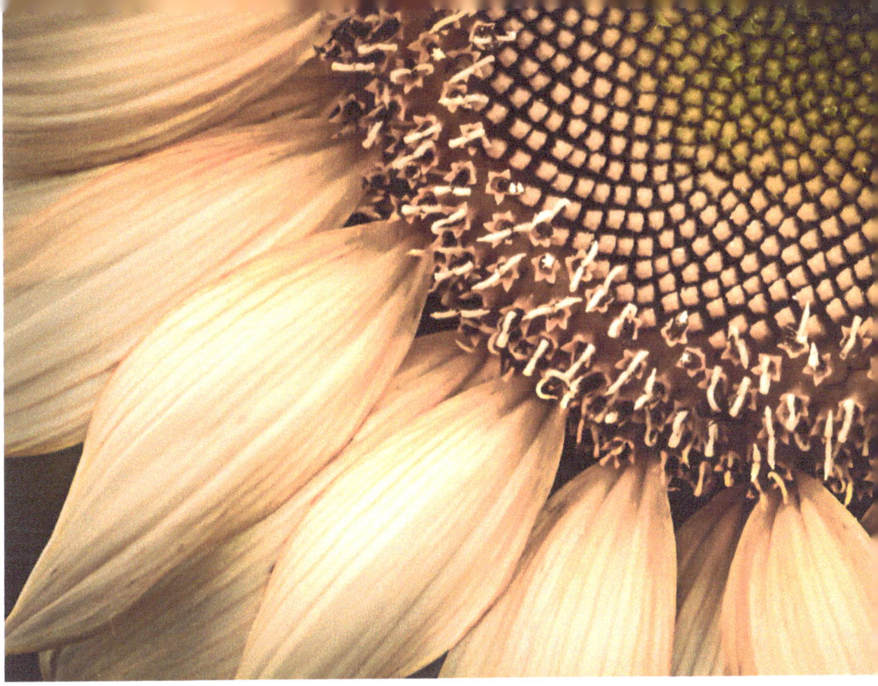

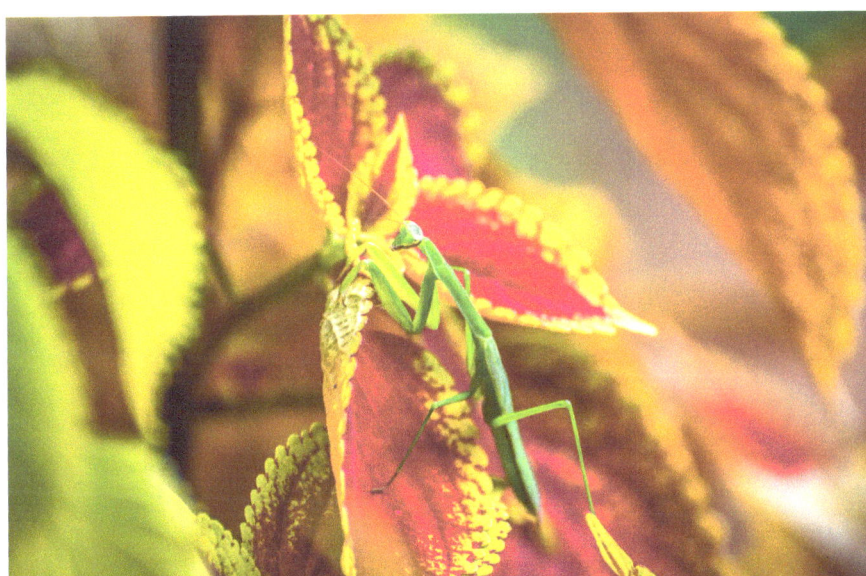

Interesting abstract effect of a macro shot of a sunflower.

cameras/lenses have different points at how close you can be and still focus, so check out your limits and get close!

Macro photography of a praying mantis on a coleus plant.

Still Life

Still life photography is a great way to practice shooting and discover your camera settings. Set up some flowers, books, or fruit bowls near a window getting indirect sunlight. Move them different directions and photograph from different directions. There is no pressure as the bowl of fruit will not whine and the books will not decide that they are done being photographed. This is where you can really take control of learning your camera.

I set up this still life to practice a photography technique called light painting, which is a method of working with a camera on a tripod in a dark room using a light source to highlight different parts of the image.

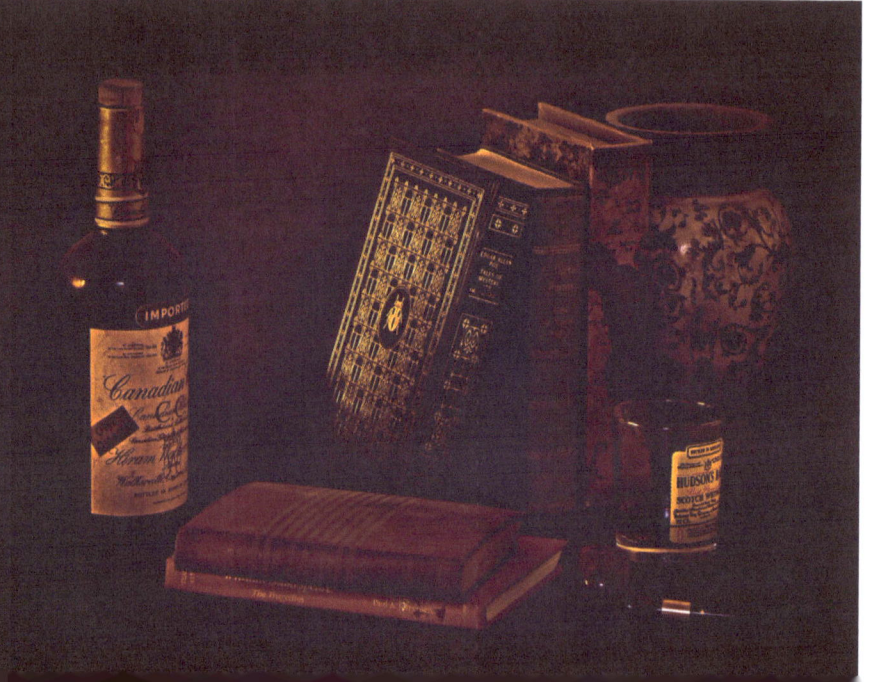

Summary

- Children – No cheesy smiles.
- Families – Create a relaxed and playful environment
- Pets – Have a wrangler and expect the unexpected.
- Sports – Use higher ISO, faster shutter speed
- Automotive – Get low, be creative!
- Landscapes – Keep that horizon straight.
- Travel – Capture "slices of life."
- Macro – Get close!
- Still Life – Great for practicing or learning new skills or settings.

Whatever subject you choose, try some of the easy tips in this book, and you will see some wonderful results!

6 • EDITING

Again, this is a topic you could read about for the rest of your life, all the way from high end software for photographers, to one click apps on your phone. In keeping with the simple theme of this book, I will just cover a few of the quick and easy aspects.

Garbage In Garbage Out

Since I am also a tech nerd, I'm tossing in a computer term because it fits. In the computer world, if you input garbled data, the output is garbled data. Well, the same is basically true for editing photos.

If you have a terrible quality photo, and put it through editing software, you will still have a terrible quality photo. Sure, you might be able to disguise it a bit, but it's going to be limited.

I believe editing should be viewed as enhancing, not repairing. If you have a stellar photo, likely it will only need minimal editing, but the effects can be dramatic. Editing can make a bad photo acceptable, but it can make a great photo spectacular. The better you begin with, the better the result.

Color vs. Black and White

Of course, both color and black and white have their place and some photos lend themselves to one or the other. Colorful photos demand attention, but, if you have a lot of color distractions in an overly busy photograph, converting it to black and white can help.

Photographer, Ted Grant once said, "When you photograph people in color, you photograph their clothes. But when you photograph people in black and white, you photograph their souls!"

This is a high key black and white portrait, taken outside in open shade, during golden hour. Brightly colored clothes and bright green background would have taken away from this sweet moment.

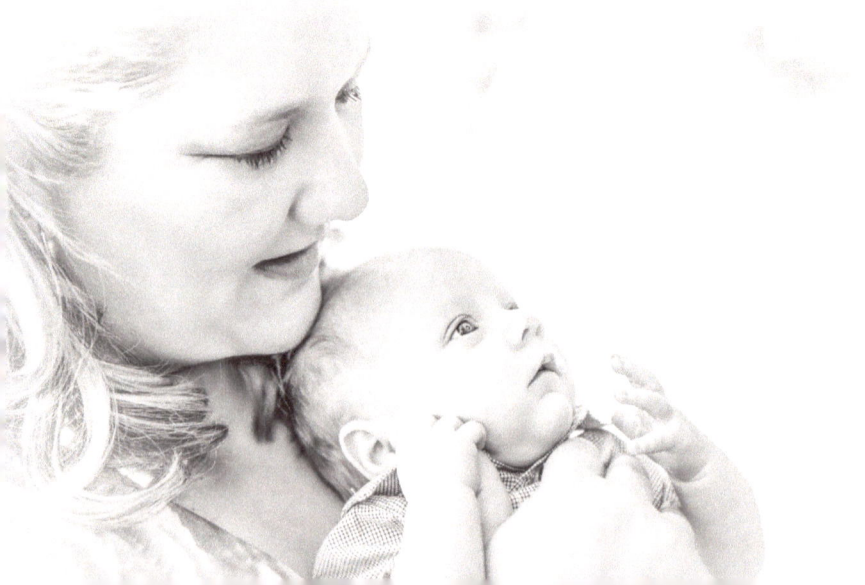

Over Editing

Especially with phone apps, there is a tendency to want to run every photograph through some sort of filter or special effect. Often these effects will take away from an otherwise nice photo. Make sure the effect you apply enhances your photo not detracts from it.

Summary

- Garbage in, garbage out.

- Try photos, particularly portraits, in black and white.

- Don't over-edit.

Remember that the better photo you have before editing, the more successful your editing will be. Edit carefully to make sure what you are doing improves your image.

7 • HELPFUL ODDS & ENDS

There are a few tips or explanations that didn't really fit in the other chapters of this book, but I felt important enough to tell you about. Here are some special situations or terms that will be useful for you to know.

HDR

Some cameras now come with an HDR setting. What does HDR stand for? It stands for High-Dynamic-Range. When you make a photo, sometimes there are very bright parts that get blown out and you loose what was in the bright spot, and/or there are very dark spots, in shadows, where things get lost in darkness.

HDR combines exposures to tone down the bright parts and lighten the dark areas so that both can be seen in the same image. As I mentioned, some cameras now have that setting, as do phones, and you can even get more sophisticated apps or software for HDR processing.

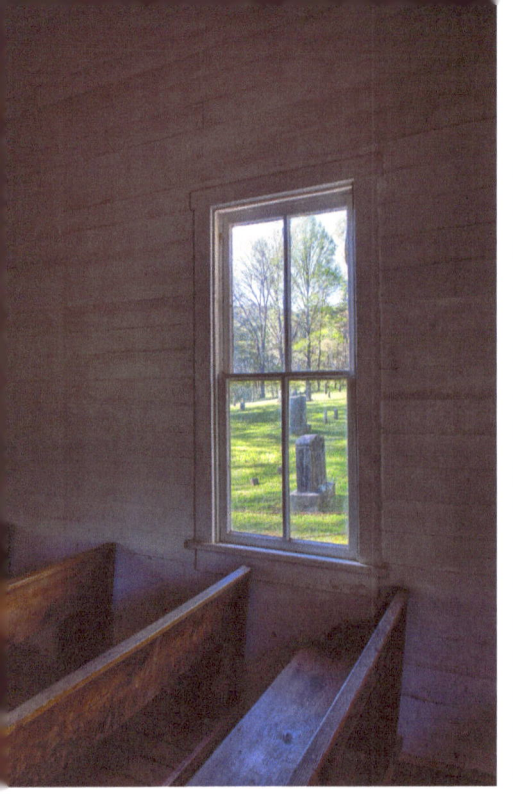

For an example of HDR photography, let's look at this photo taken inside the Methodist Church in Cades Cove, TN. It is a dark room (no lights) with a visible window. If you lighten the room to correct exposure, where you can clearly see inside, the light from the windows gets way too bright and just looks white. Conversely, if you darken the photo to the point where the view out of the windows is correct, the room is too dark. HDR is a way to handle those problems.

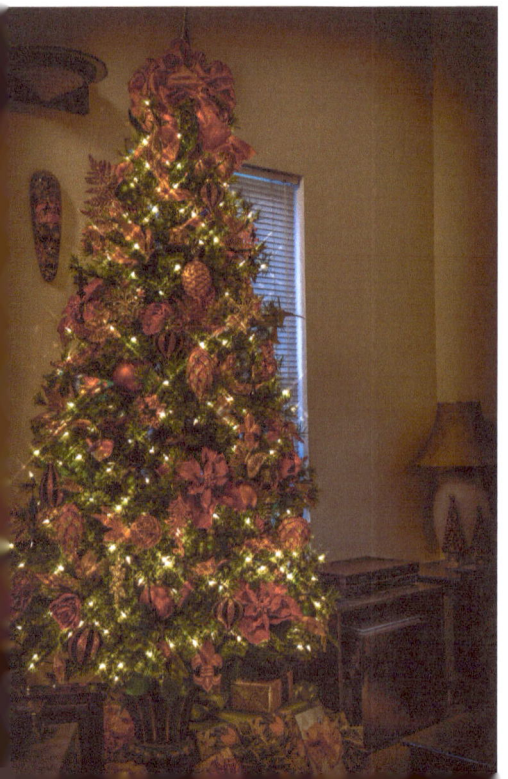

Because I'm a Christmas freak, I am including this example of HDR photography. Note the bright spots are toned town and the dark shadows are lightened.

Shooting From a Moving Vehicle

I tagged along on a breakneck trip from East Tennessee to Dallas, Texas a few years ago, because, of course, I wanted the opportunity to take pictures. The problem was, that in order to make the trip in the allotted time, there was no time for sightseeing. Most of what I would be photographing would be from the window of the truck.

What did I learn? I learned that to get photos that weren't ugly blurs of the roadside, I needed to move my shutter speed up. In fact, when I travel (and I'm not driving), I make a lot of photographs along the way. Some shots you just can't get anywhere else, such as views off the side of a mountain road, especially when there is no shoulder of the road to even pull over, out of the traffic flow.

If you are trying to shoot from a moving vehicle, definitely set your shutter speed up. I like to start with about 1/1000 of a second and adjust from there.

Shooting Through Glass

What else did I learn on the trip to Texas? Because it was in January, I learned some things about shooting through glass because other people in the vehicle don't particularly appreciate the window down at 60mph in January so you can make a picture.

Different glass has different tints, even if you think it looks clear. Some tends to have a blue or greenish hue sometimes that can be adjusted in editing, usually in a section pertaining to white balance.

Also, sometimes you just have to roll down the window. The angle of the glass sometimes can really screw up your photo. If the camera focuses on the glass instead of the subject outside, you will end up with blurry images. This happens more if you are seeing a reflection on the glass. Your camera will see it, too, and try to focus in the wrong place.

If you are in a non-mobile environment, such as at a zoo or aquarium where there is glass, try to get

This photo of the Great Smoky Mountains was taken from a moving vehicle, through the windshield going East on I-40 in Cocke County, TN.

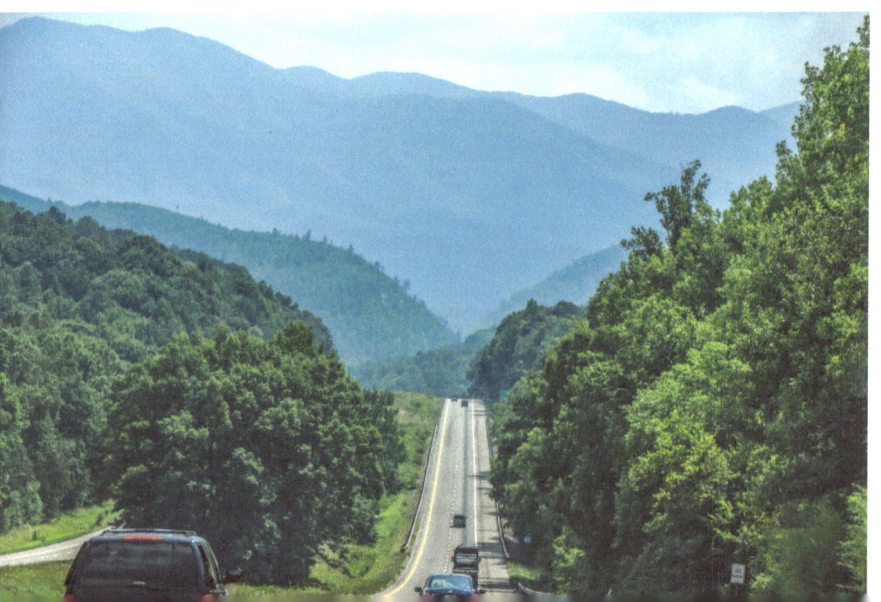

as close as possible without banging your camera and make sure you aren't at an angle where there is a reflection.

Shooting through glass is difficult, so if there is another way (that won't potentially get you thrown from a moving vehicle) to get the shot, I'd suggest giving it a try.

Summary

- HDR is helpful when you have extreme contrasts of light and dark
- Move shutter speed up when shooting from a moving vehicle.
- Clear glass sometimes has a blue or green tint.
- Watch out for reflections and glares when shooting through glass.

Having tools and skills to adjust to whatever situation you find yourself with your camera will help you get those shots that no one else can get. Practice these techniques and impress everyone with your newfound abilities.

8 • YOUR TURN

Now that you have this whole new arsenal of photography tricks, it's time for you to go out and use them. I know you will see an immediate difference in your images. You now have tools to capture the special moments of your family and friends in a more professional and meaningful way.

I have included a simple Quick Reference chart and a link that you can access online, and save to your phone when you need an answer fast, and don't have this book with you. I wish you much success in your photo making endeavors (gee, this feels like I'm signing your yearbook, doesn't it?). But I really do want the photos of your family to be treasures you can pass down proudly.

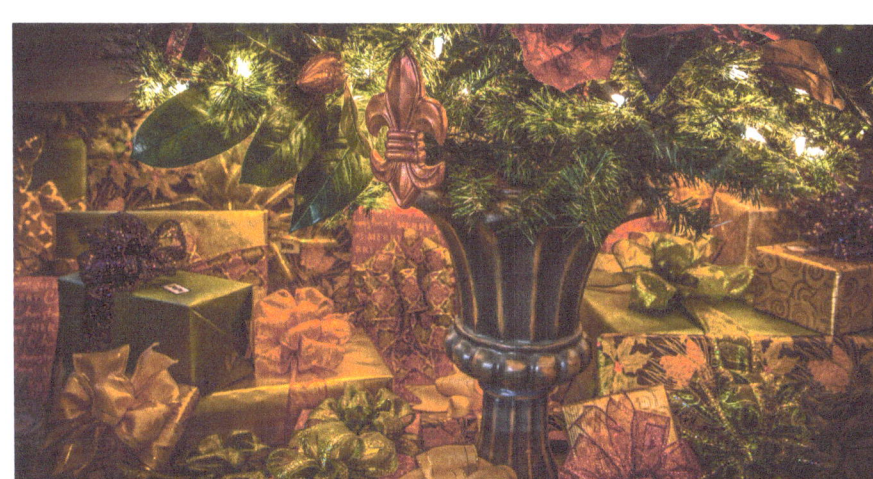

QUICK REFERENCE CHART

The following chart is available for download as a .pdf at the following link: www.hoipolloiphotography.com/chart.html

Cameras	DSLR	· moveable mirror
	DSLT	· fixed translucent mirror
	Point & Shoot	· most common (exc cell phones) · easy to use
	Camera Phone	· some now have advanced features
Zoom	Digital Zoom	· not true zoom · only enlarging
	Optical Zoom	· true zoom · uses optics
Photographic Triangle	ISO	· sensitivity to light (film speed) · higher number = more noise, grain
	Aperture	· size of the opening of the lens · smaller number = wider opening
	Shutter Speed	· how fast the shutter opens and closes
Composition	Rule of Thirds	· tic-tac-toe grid · place subjects at intersections
	Horizon Lines	· keep level · put on upper or lower third lines · do not dead center unless intended
	Keep Simple	· move closer to subject · use wider aperture to blur background
	Eyes	· keep in focus
	Subjects	· give them room to move or look
	Framing	· look for ways to frame your photo
	Leading Lines	· draw your viewer into the photo
	Bokeh	· blur of light using wider aperture
Lighting (Photography is the study of light)	Natural Light	· requires less equipment · place subject in open shade · use umbrella to diffuse light · avoid dappled light
	Flash	· use outdoors to soften harsh shadows in bright sunlight
	Golden Hour	· the hour after sunrise and before sunset · great, warm light
	Blue Hour	· the hour before sunrise and after sunset · nice time for night shots
Subjects	Children	· no cheesy smiles
	Families	· have parents hold little ones and walk for group photos
	Pets	· have a wrangler · expect the unexpected
	Sports	· use higher ISO · use faster shutter speed
	Automotive	· get low · shoot iconic parts · be creative
	Landscapes	· keep horizon level
	Travel	· capture slices of life
	Macro	· get close!
	Still Life	· great for practicing new skills
Editing	Garbage In Garbage Out	· starting with better photos yields better results
	Try Photos in Black & White	· experiment with color and b&w · try portraits in b&w
	Don't Over-Edit	· keep effects to a minimum
Odds & Ends	HDR	· combines exposures so bright and dark areas can be seen
	Shooting from Moving Vehicle	· move shutter speed up
	Shooting through Glass	· watch out for reflections · sometimes has a blue or green tint

ABOUT THE AUTHOR

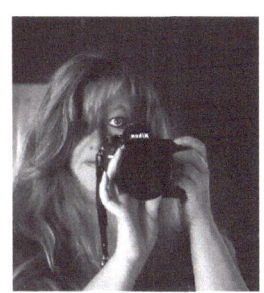

April Bryant is the owner of HPP Media & Design, encompassing April Bryant Photography, Hoi Polloi Photography, and the online newspaper, *Nolichucky Guardian,* where she is also editor, and a member of the US Press Association.

She has been creating since she was old enough to hold a crayon. She enjoys classical drawing and painting, as well as calligraphy, but her true passion is photography. Trained as an IT Professional, she enjoys combining artistic talents with technical skills to create interesting and intriguing works of fine art. She also likes the challenges of graphic design, compositing, and web design.

She is a photography contributor to the prestigious Getty Images, and was chosen as a First Collection Contributor for 500Prime, a commercial photography agency. She has also had work published by the Sierra Club. She is a member of The Arts & Culture Alliance of Greater Knoxville, Tennessee.

Two of her photographs received awards in the 2015 Open Art Exhibition hosted by Light Space & Time Online Gallery.

She has two sons, Fletcher, 21, and Jesse, 14, who are also very artistic. When she isn't out with her camera, she enjoys organic gardening and working with her rescue cat, Gracie.

Shameless Plug... If you would like to contact her for photography services, compositing, graphic, or web design, you may contact her at *info@hoipolloi-photography.com* or visit her websites:

www.HoiPolloiPhotography.com

www.AprilBryant.com

www.NolichuckyGuardian.com